I0170577

Music Rhythm Worksheets

Beginning
Through Intermediate
Studies

ANNETTE MACKEY

MP

This publication is protected by Copyright. The notice at the bottom of each page must be included on educational copies. Copies that do not contain the notice are in violation of Copyright law and subject to prosecution.

The opinions expressed in this work are solely the opinion of the author/composer. The author/composer has represented and warranted full ownership and/or legal right to publish all the materials in this book.

Music Rhythm Worksheets
All Rights Reserved
Copyright 2013 Annette Mackey

This book may not be reproduced, transmitted, or stored in whole or in part by any means, including graphic, electronic, or mechanical without the express written consent of the publisher except in accordance with the written notice at the bottom of individual worksheets. All worksheets must retain the Copyright notice or they are in violation of Copyright law. Brief quotations embodied in critical articles and reviews are permitted.

Mandolin Publishing
Boise, Idaho

ISBN: 978-0-9836104-3-4
Mandolin Publishing and the "MP" logo are trademarks belonging to Mandolin Publishing.
Printed in the United States of America

An understanding of rhythm is one of the most important factors in a musician's ability to sight read. It is also a major factor in becoming an independent musician. Unfortunately there are few resources available to students in this area. That is why I created these worksheets. It is my hope that this unit will aid teachers in the instruction process. As such, I have included a notice on each worksheet, which allows them to be copied for noncommercial educational use **AFTER the initial purchase of the unit.** Copies made by those who have not purchased the unit are in violation of Copyright law. Worksheets that do not contain the Copyright notice are in violation of Copyright law.

~Annette Mackey

Table of Contents

Basic Beginning Rhythm

Beginning Rhythm

Introduction to Intermediate Rhythm

Table of Contents (Cont.)

Intermediate Rhythm

Introduction to Compound Rhythm

Introducing Quarter and Half Notes
Worksheet 1.0

Quarter notes receive one count. Clap and count them.

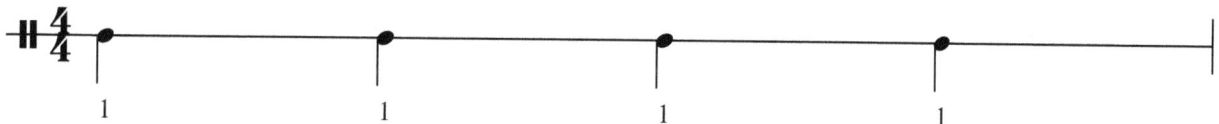

Half notes receive two counts. Clap and count them.

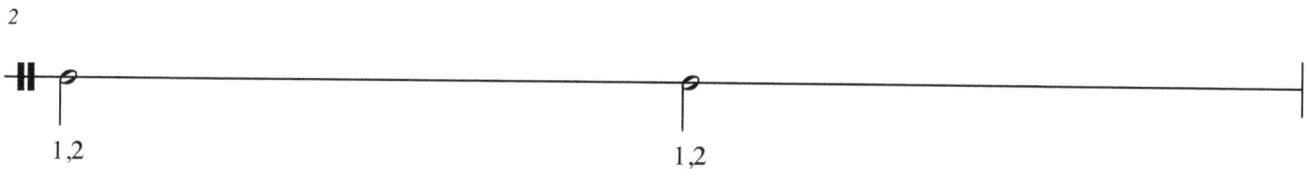

Quarter notes and half notes. Clap and count.

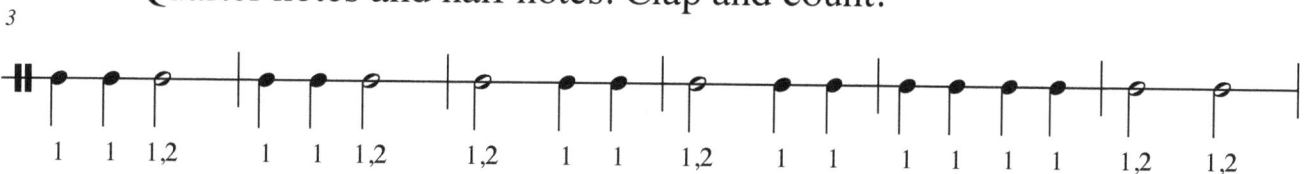

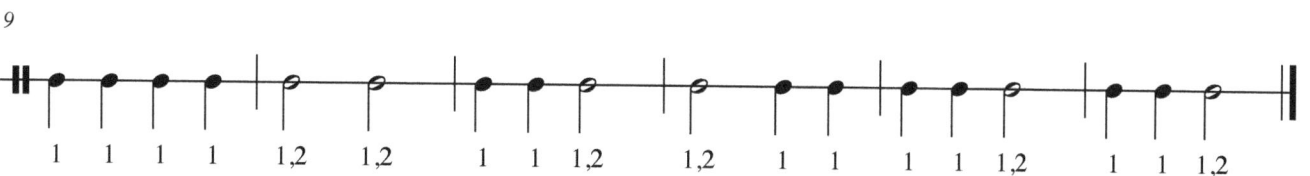

Copyright 2013 by Annette Mackey. AFTER INITIAL PURCHASE a copy may be made for educational, non-commercial use. All copies must contain this notice. http://www.annettemackey.com

Time Signatures

Notice that at the top left hand corner of the music are the numbers 4 / 4 stacked over the top of one another. This is not a fraction. This is the time signature. The top number tells us how many counts are in each measure. The bottom number tells us what kind of note receives one count. From now on, we will count music within time signatures.

A four on the top means that there are four counts in each measure.

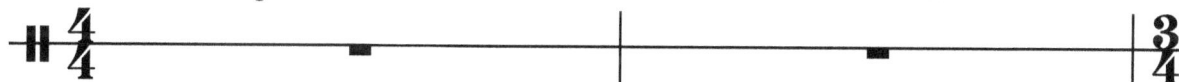

A four on the bottom means that the quarter note will receive one count.

Upcoming time signature changes which occur at the beginning of the next line are marked in advance.

A three on the top means that there are three counts in each measure.

Four is still on the bottom, so the quarter note will receive one count.

A two on the top means that there are two counts in each measure.

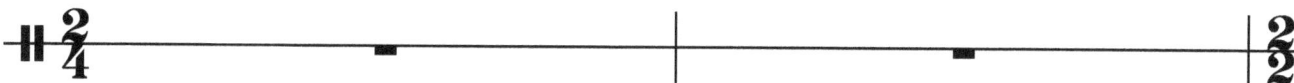

Four is still on the bottom, so the quarter note will receive one count.

Again we have a two on the top. There are two counts in each measure.

Now two is on the bottom, so a half note will receive one count.

Six is on the top. There are six counts in each measure.

Eight is on the bottom. The eighth note will receive one count.

Copyright 2013 by Annette Mackey. AFTER INITIAL PURCHASE a copy may be made for educational, non-commercial use. All copies must contain this notice. http://www.annettemackey.com

Dotted Half Notes and Quarter Rest
Worksheet 1.2

Dotted half notes get three counts. Clap and Count.

1,2,3

2 Half notes and quarter notes.

1,2,3   1,2   3   1,2   3   1,2,3

6 Quarter rests get one count. Snap on the rests.

1   2   3

Let's mix it all together: Clap and count, snap on the rests.
Quarter notes, quarter rests, dotted half notes, and half notes.

7

1   2   3   1   2   3   1,2   3   1   2,3

11

1   2   3   1,2,3   1,2,3   1   2   3

Copyright 2013 by Annette Mackey. AFTER INITIAL PURCHASE a copy may be made for educational, non-commercial use. All copies must contain this notice. http://www.annettemackey.com

Beginning Rhythm in Common Time
Worksheet 1.3

Counting in 4 / 4 time. Each measure must add up to four counts.
Clap and count the notes. Snap on the rests.

Copyright 2013 by Annette Mackey. AFTER INITIAL PURCHASE a copy may be made for educational, non-commercial use. All copies must contain this notice. http://www.annettemackey.com

Beginning Rhythm in 3 / 4 Time
Worksheet 1.4

Clap and count the notes. Snap on the rests.

Copyright 2013 by Annette Mackey. AFTER INITIAL PURCHASE a copy may be made for educational, non-commercial use. All copies must contain this notice. http://www.annettemackey.com

Quarter, Half, Whole, Notes and Rests
Worksheet 2.0

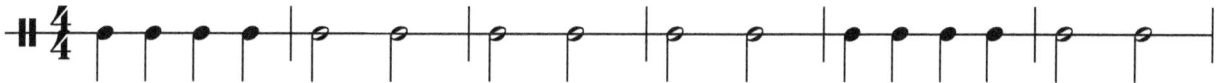

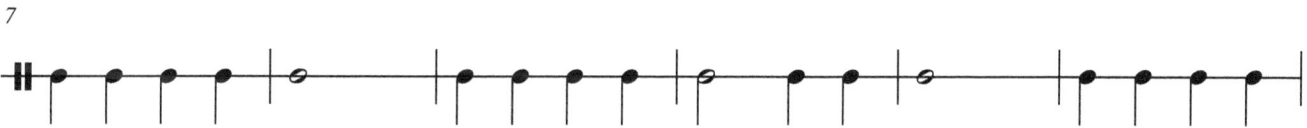

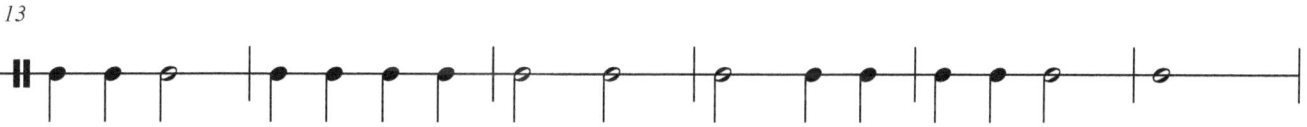

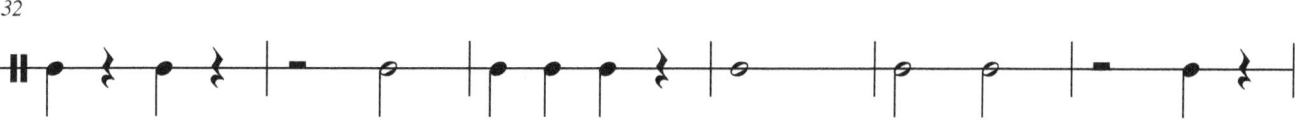

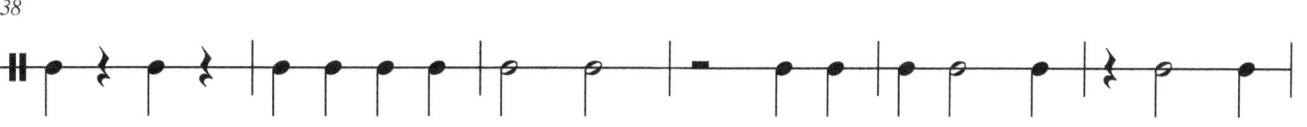

Copyright 2013 by Annette Mackey. AFTER INITIAL PURCHASE a copy may be made for educational, non-commercial use. All copies must contain this notice. http://www.annettemackey.com

Quarter, Half, Dotted Half, Whole
Notes and Rests
Worksheet 2.1

6

12

18

25

31

37

43

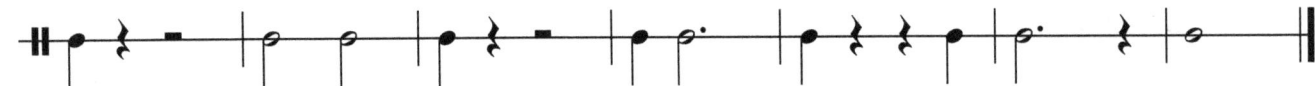

Copyright 2013 by Annette Mackey. AFTER INITIAL PURCHASE a copy may be made for educational, non-commercial use. All copies must contain this notice. http://www.annettemackey.com

Quarter, Half, Dotted Half, Whole
Notes, Ties, and Rests
Worksheet 2.2

7

14

21

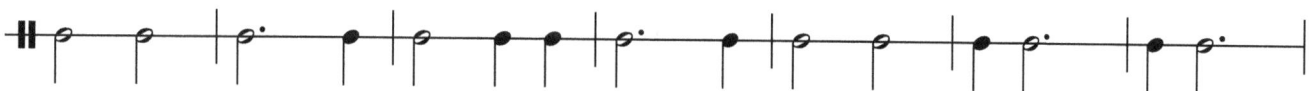

28

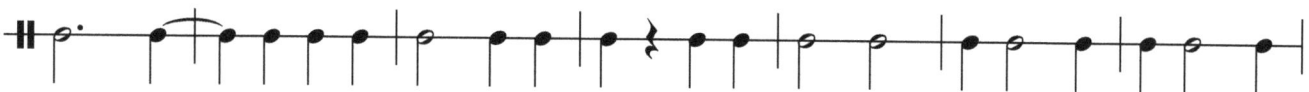

35

42

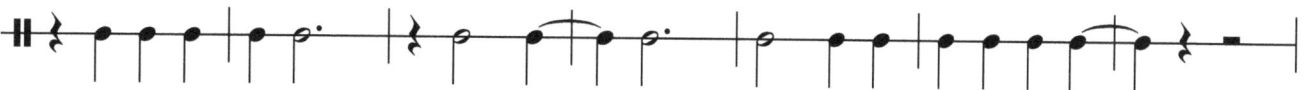

49

Copyright 2013 by Annette Mackey. AFTER INITIAL PURCHASE a copy may be made for educational, non-commercial use. All copies must contain this notice. http://www.annettemackey.com

Quarter, Half, Dotted Half, Whole Notes, Ties, and Rests, Additional Practice Worksheet 2.3

Copyright 2013 by Annette Mackey. AFTER INITIAL PURCHASE a copy may be made for educational, non-commercial use. All copies must contain this notice. http://www.annettemackey.com

Quarter, Half, Dotted Half, Whole Notes, Ties, and Rests, Additional Practice Worksheet 2.4

Copyright 2013 by Annette Mackey. AFTER INITIAL PURCHASE a copy may be made for educational, non-commercial use. All copies must contain this notice. http://www.annettemackey.com

Quarter, Half, and Whole Notes
Worksheet 1.1

Whole notes receive four counts. Clap and count.

1,2,3,4

Half notes receive two counts. Clap and count.

1,2   1,2

Quarter notes receive one count. Clap and count.

1   1   1   1

Let's mix them up. Clap and count.

1 1 1,2   1,2,3,4   1 1 1,2   1,2,3,4   1,2   1,2   1,2   1 1

1 1 1 1   1,2,3,4   1 1 1,2   1 1 1 1   1,2,3,4

Copyright 2013 by Annette Mackey. AFTER INITIAL PURCHASE a copy may be made for educational, non-commercial use. All copies must contain this notice. http://www.annettemackey.com

Quarter, Half, Dotted Half, Whole
Notes, Ties, and Rests, Additional Practice
Worksheet 2.5

Copyright 2013 by Annette Mackey. AFTER INITIAL PURCHASE a copy may be made for educational, non-commercial use. All copies must contain this notice. http://www.annettemackey.com

Quarter, Half, Dotted Half, Whole Notes, Ties, and Rests, Additional Practice Worksheet 2.6

Copyright 2013 by Annette Mackey. AFTER INITIAL PURCHASE a copy may be made for educational, non-commercial use. All copies must contain this notice. http://www.annettemackey.com

Quarter, Half, Dotted Half, Whole Notes, Ties, and Rests, Additional Practice Worksheet 2.7

Copyright 2013 by Annette Mackey. AFTER INITIAL PURCHASE a copy may be made for educational, non-commercial use. All copies must contain this notice. http://www.annettemackey.com

Quarter, Half, Dotted Half, Whole
Notes, Ties, and Rests in 3 / 4 Time
Worksheet 2.8

Copyright 2013 by Annette Mackey. AFTER INITIAL PURCHASE a copy may be made for educational, non-commercial use. All copies must contain this notice. http://www.annettemackey.com

Quarter, Half, Dotted Half, Whole
Notes, Ties, and Rests in 3 / 4 Time, Additional Practice
Worksheet 2.9

Copyright 2013 by Annette Mackey. AFTER INITIAL PURCHASE a copy may be made for educational, non-commercial use. All copies must contain this notice. http://www.annettemackey.com

Introducing Eighth Notes
Worksheet 2.10

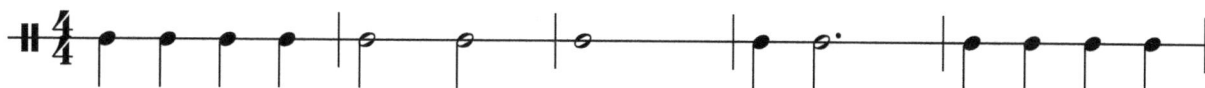

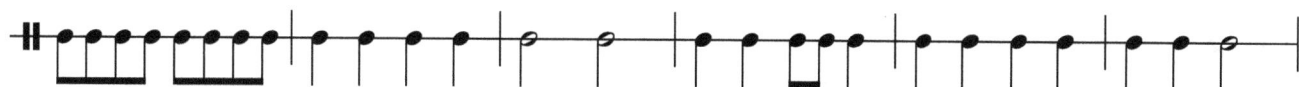

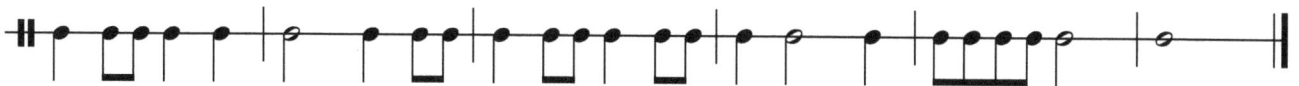

Copyright 2013 by Annette Mackey. AFTER INITIAL PURCHASE a copy may be made for educational, non-commercial use. All copies must contain this notice. http://www.annettemackey.com

Introducing Eighth Rests
Worksheet 2.11

Copyright 2013 by Annette Mackey. AFTER INITIAL PURCHASE a copy may be made for educational, non-commercial use. All copies must contain this notice. http://www.annettemackey.com

A Brief Explanation of Dotted Notes

The following equation may be used to determine dotted note values.
Take the NOTE VALUE and add HALF of the NOTE VALUE to equal the DOTTED NOTE VALUE.

(half note) + (half of half note is quarter note) =

+ =

2 counts (half note value) + 1 count (half of half note value) = 3

1 + 1/2 = 1 1/2

1,2,3,4   1,2,3,4

3

1,2   3,4   1,2   3,4

5

1   2   3   4   1   2   3   4

Music "spacing" does not alter the rhythm of the music. Even though the beats in the line below do not
7 line up precisely with the line above, the rhythmic location of the beats remains constant.

1,2,3,   4   1   2,3,4

9

1   2   3   4   1   2   3   4

11

1 & 2 & 3 & 4 &   1 & 2 & 3 & 4 &

13

1 & 2 & 3 & 4 1 2 3 & 4 &

Copyright 2013 by Annette Mackey. AFTER INITIAL PURCHASE a copy may be made for educational, non-commercial use. All copies must contain this notice. http://www.annettemackey.com

Dotted Quarter Note Followed By Eighth Note
Worksheet 2.12

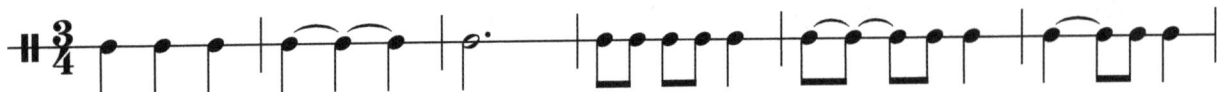

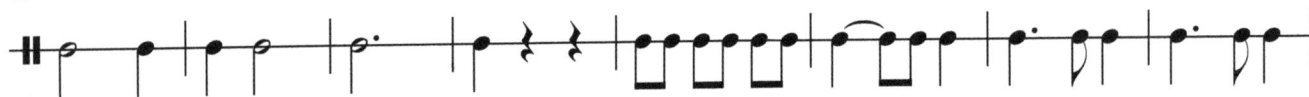

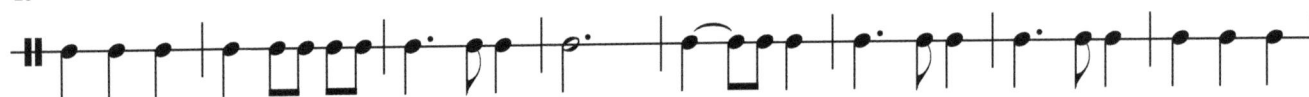

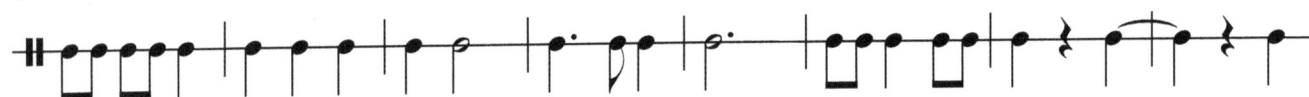

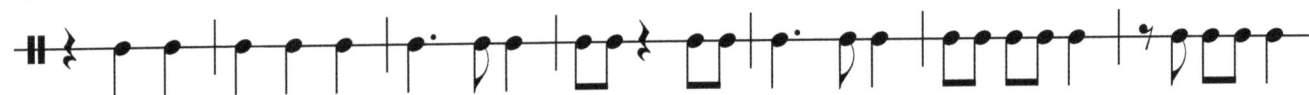

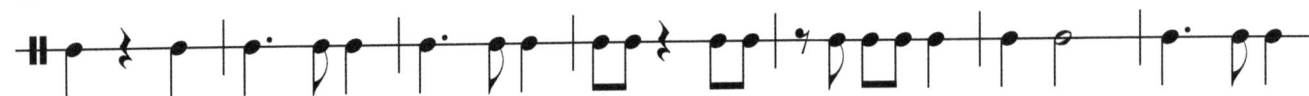

Copyright 2013 by Annette Mackey. AFTER INITIAL PURCHASE a copy may be made for educational, non-commercial use. All copies must contain this notice. http://www.annettemackey.com

Dotted Quarter Note Followed By Eighth Note
Additional Practice
Worksheet 2.13

6

12

18

25

36

47

54

Copyright 2013 by Annette Mackey. AFTER INITIAL PURCHASE a copy may be made for educational, non-commercial use. All copies must contain this notice. http://www.annettemackey.com

Dotted Quarter Note Followed by Eighth Note
Additional Practice
Worksheet 2.14

Copyright 2013 by Annette Mackey. AFTER INITIAL PURCHASE a copy may be made for educational, non-commercial use. All copies must contain this notice. http://www.annettemackey.com

Dotted Quarter Note Followed by Eighth Note
Additional Practice
Worksheet 2.15

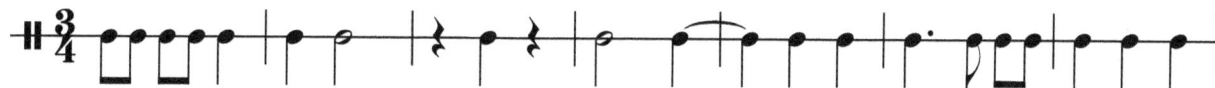

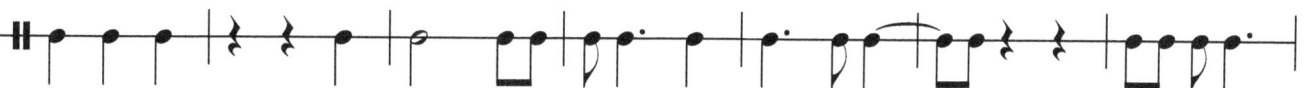

Copyright 2013 by Annette Mackey. AFTER INITIAL PURCHASE a copy may be made for educational, non-commercial use. All copies must contain this notice. http://www.annettemackey.com

Eighth Note Triplets
Worksheet 2.16

3 eighth note triplets equal the same amount of time as 1 quarter note.

Copyright 2013 by Annette Mackey. AFTER INITIAL PURCHASE a copy may be made for educational, non-commercial use. All copies must contain this notice. http://www.annettemackey.com

Eighth Note Triplets, Additional Practice
Worksheet 2.17

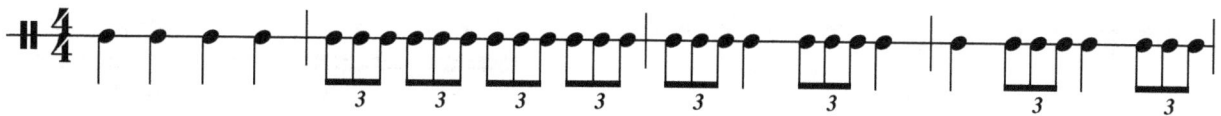

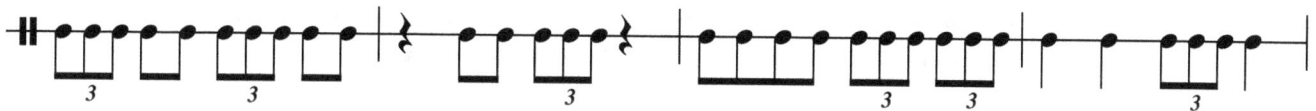

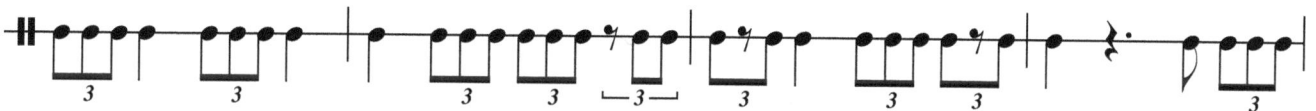

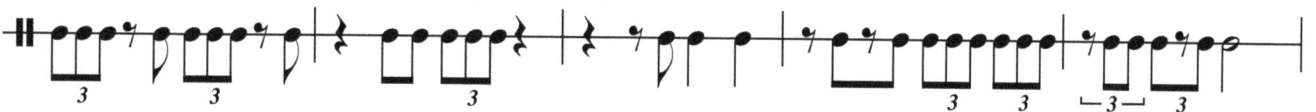

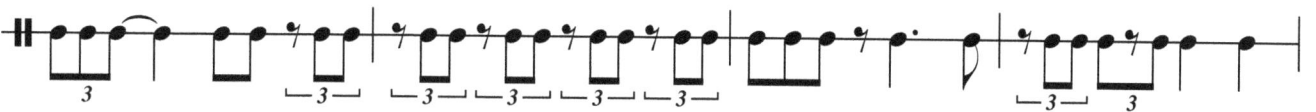

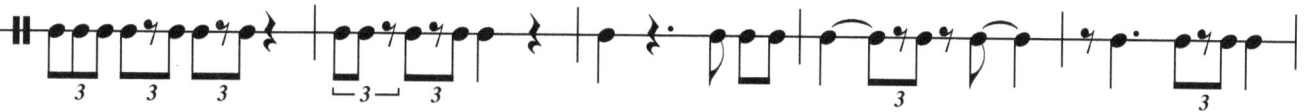

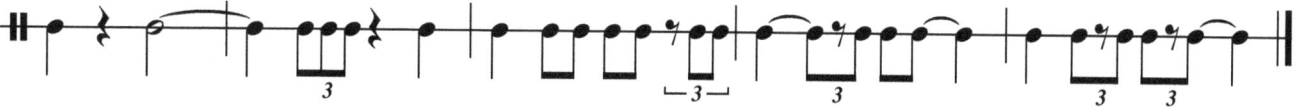

Copyright 2013 by Annette Mackey. AFTER INITIAL PURCHASE a copy may be made for educational, non-commercial use. All copies must contain this notice. http://www.annettemackey.com

Beginning Sixteenth Notes
Worksheet 3.0

In 4 / 4 time there are 4 quarter notes per measure, 8 eighth notes, and 16 sixteenth notes.

Repeat as necessary for understanding of note relationships

Copyright 2013 by Annette Mackey. AFTER INITIAL PURCHASE a copy may be made for educational, non-commercial use. All copies must contain this notice. http://www.annettemackey.com

Sixteenth Notes, Additional Practice
Worksheet 3.1

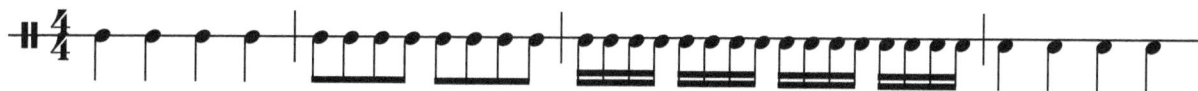

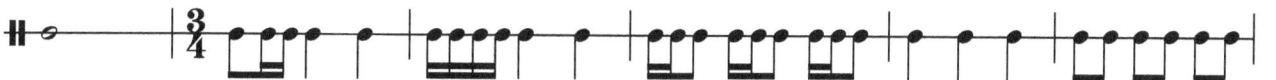

Copyright 2013 by Annette Mackey. AFTER INITIAL PURCHASE a copy may be made for educational, non-commercial use. All copies must contain this notice. http://www.annettemackey.com

Sixteenth Notes, Additional Practice
Worksheet 3.2

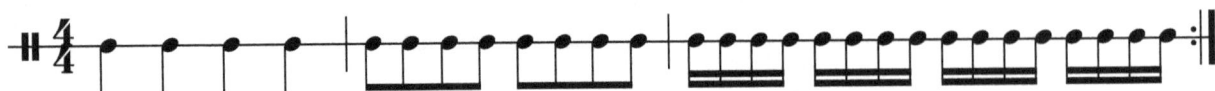

4

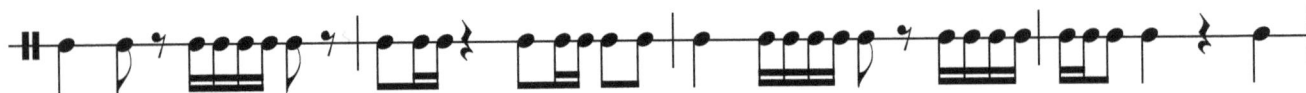

8

11

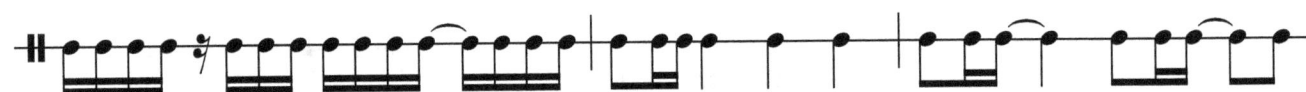

14

18

22

26

Copyright 2013 by Annette Mackey. AFTER INITIAL PURCHASE a copy may be made for educational, non-commercial use. All copies must contain this notice. http://www.annettemackey.com

Combining Concepts
Sixteenth, Eighth, Quarter, Half, Whole, Dotted
Worksheet 3.3

Keep an even tempo. To avoid problems go slowly at first.
It is more important to be accurate than to be fast.

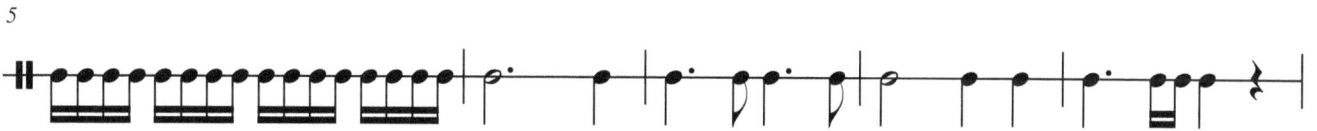

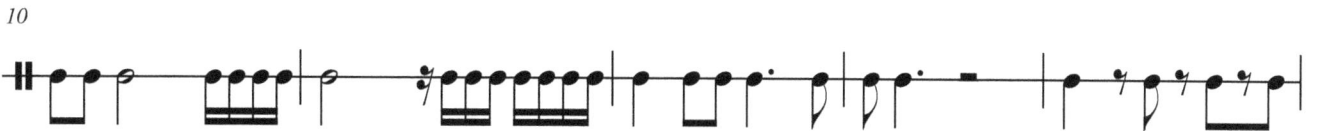

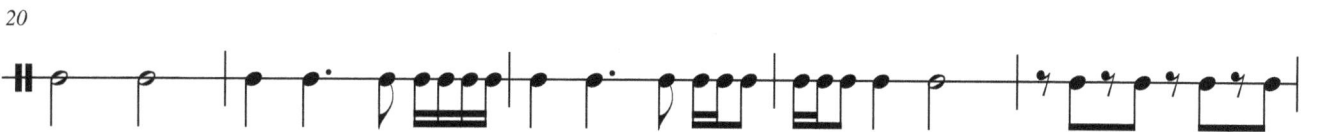

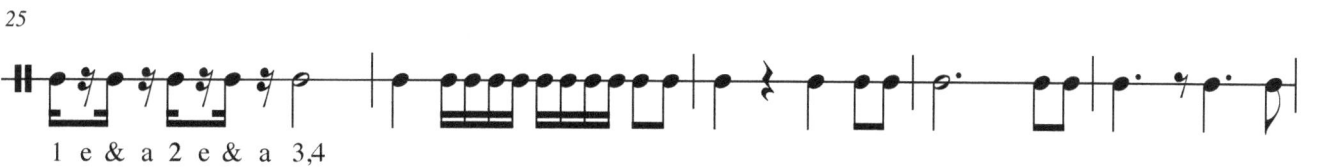

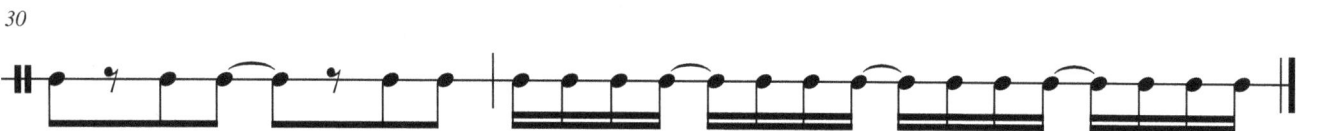

1 e & a 2 e & a 3,4

Copyright 2013 by Annette Mackey. AFTER INITIAL PURCHASE a copy may be made for educational, non-commercial use. All copies must contain this notice. http://www.annettemackey.com

Combining Concepts
Additional Practice, Count As Marked
Worksheet 3.4

Copyright 2013 by Annette Mackey. AFTER INITIAL PURCHASE a copy may be made for educational, non-commercial use. All copies must contain this notice. http://www.annettemackey.com

Dotted Sixteenth Notes and Rests
Worksheet 3.5

4

8

12

1 e & 2 & a 3 e & 4 & a 1 e &,2 & a 3 e &,4 & a

16

20

1 e & a 2 e &,a 3e,&,a 4,e,& a 1 e & a,2 e &,a 3,e,&,a 4,e,& a

23

1 & 2 & 3 e & 4 1 &,2 & 3 e & 4

27

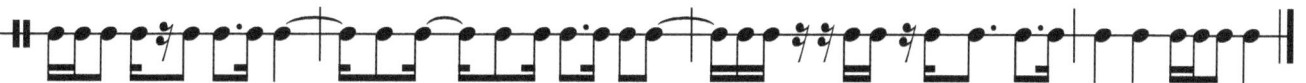

1 e & 2 e & 3 a 4 1 e,& a 2 e,& a 3 a 4 a 1 e & a 2 e & a 3 e,&,a 4 a

Copyright 2013 by Annette Mackey. AFTER INITIAL PURCHASE a copy may be made for educational, non-commercial use. All copies must contain this notice. http://www.annettemackey.com

Half Note Receiving One Beat
Worksheet 3.6

The following are examples of time signatures with a 2 on the bottom,
meaning that the half note receives one beat. 2 / 2 time is counted the same as cut time.
Beginning at measure 20 the time signature will change frequently.

Dotted half notes receive one and a half counts

Copyright 2013 by Annette Mackey. AFTER INITIAL PURCHASE a copy may be made for educational, non-commercial use. All copies must contain this notice. http://www.annettemackey.com

Sixteenth Note and Eighth Note Triplets
Worksheet 3.7

Copyright 2013 by Annette Mackey. AFTER INITIAL PURCHASE a copy may be made for educational, non-commercial use. All copies must contain this notice. http://www.annettemackey.com

Quarter Note Triplets
Worksheet 3.8

3 quarter note triplets equal the same amount of time as 1 half note.

Copyright 2013 by Annette Mackey. AFTER INITIAL PURCHASE a copy may be made for educational, non-commercial use. All copies must contain this notice. http://www.annettemackey.com

Combining Concepts with Triplets
Worksheet 3.9

5

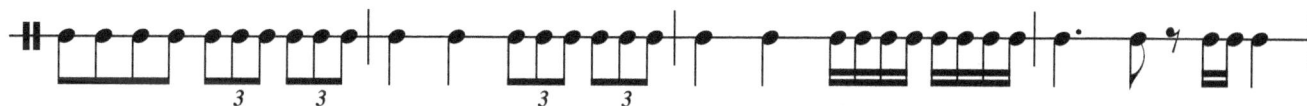

9

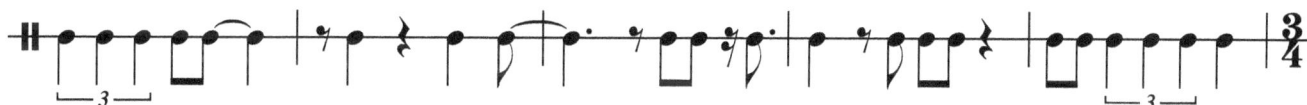

14

20

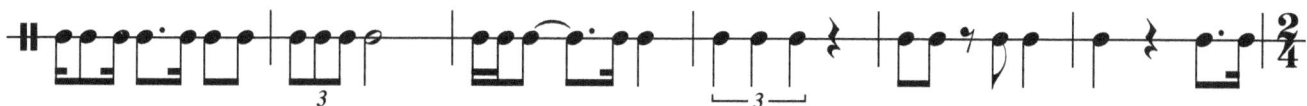

26

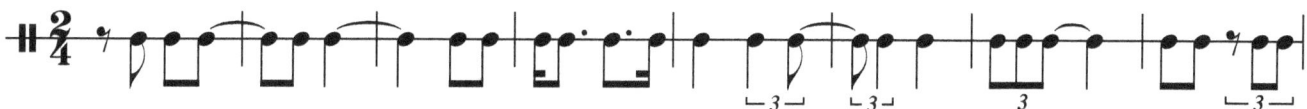

34

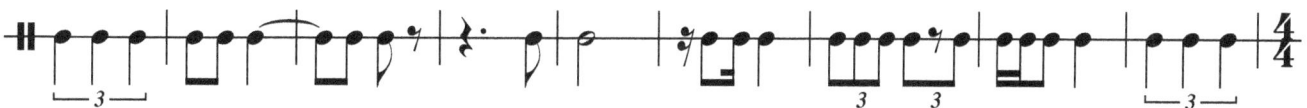

43

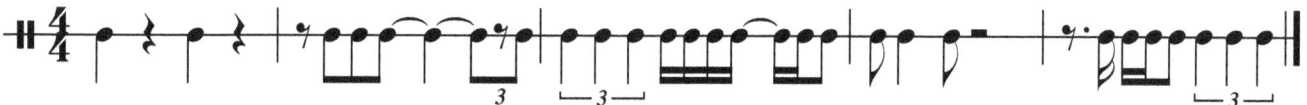

Copyright 2013 by Annette Mackey. AFTER INITIAL PURCHASE a copy may be made for educational, non-commercial use. All copies must contain this notice. http://www.annettemackey.com

Triplets, Additional Practice
Worksheet 3.10

Copyright 2013 by Annette Mackey. AFTER INITIAL PURCHASE a copy may be made for educational, non-commercial use. All copies must contain this notice. http://www.annettemackey.com

Intermediate Rhythm, Additional Practice
Worksheet 3.11

Copyright 2013 by Annette Mackey. AFTER INITIAL PURCHASE a copy may be made for educational, non-commercial use. All copies must contain this notice. http://www.annettemackey.com

A Brief Explanation of Compound Time
3 / 8, 6 / 8, 9 / 8, and 12 / 8

Compound time is notorious for confusing students. Compound Time consists of any time signature with an 8 on the bottom. It is not necessarily more complicated. Just remember that in compound time, music is based upon THREE. There are three eighth notes per dotted quarter note. This is why the eighth notes are beamed in sets of three. In contrast, simple time is based upon TWO, with two eighth notes per quarter note. At first it may seem that these systems are the same. They are not. The difference lies in the strong beats. In simple time, the strong beat is divisible by two. In compound time, the strong beat is divisible by three. You MUST NOT attempt to turn 6 / 8 time into 3 / 4 time because time signatures are NOT fractions. They are indications of where rhythmic stress is located. See the break-out for each time signature below.

3 / 8 time: There are three eighth notes per measure with ONE strong beat per measure. It may be counted as follows:

1, 2, 3

or

1 & a (Or as instructed by your teacher.)

6 / 8 time: There are six eighth notes per measure with TWO strong beats per measure. It may be counted as follows:

1, 2, 3, 4, 5, 6

or

1 & a, 2 & a

9 / 8 time: There are nine eighth notes per measure with THREE strong beats per measure. It may be counted as follows:

1, 2, 3, 4, 5, 6, 7, 8, 9

or

1 & a, 2 & a, 3 & a

12 / 8 time: There are twelve eighth notes per measure with FOUR strong beats per measure. It may be counted as follows:

1, 2, 3, 4, 5, 6, 7, 8, 9, 10, 11, 12

or

1 & a, 2 & a, 3 & a, 4 & a

Copyright 2013 by Annette Mackey. AFTER INITIAL PURCHASE a copy may be made for educational, non-commercial use. All copies must contain this notice. http://www.annettemackey.com

A Brief Explanation of Compound Time
3 / 8, 6 / 8, 9 / 8, and 12 / 8

3 / 8 time: There are three eighth notes per measure with one strong beat per measure. It may be counted as follows: 1, 2, 3, OR 1 & a. (Or as instructed by your teacher.)

6 / 8 time: There are six eighth notes per measure with two strong beats per measure. It may be counted as: 1, 2, 3, 4, 5, 6, OR 1 & a, 2 & a.

9 / 8 time: There are nine eighth notes per measure with three strong beats per measure. It may be counted as: 1, 2, 3, 4, 5, 6, 7, 8, 9, OR 1 & a, 2 & a, 3 & a.

12 / 8 time: There are twelve eighth notes per measure with four strong beats per measure. It may be counted as: 1, 2, 3, 4, 5, 6, 7, 8, 9, 10, 11, 12, OR 1 & a, 2 & a, 3 & a, 4 & a.

Copyright 2013 by Annette Mackey. AFTER INITIAL PURCHASE a copy may be made for educational, non-commercial use. All copies must contain this notice. http://www.annettemackey.com

Beginning Compound Time
Worksheet 4.0

Copyright 2013 by Annette Mackey. AFTER INITIAL PURCHASE a copy may be made for educational, non-commercial use. All copies must contain this notice. http://www.annettemackey.com

Introducing 6 / 8 Time
Worksheet 4.1

Copyright 2013 by Annette Mackey. AFTER INITIAL PURCHASE a copy may be made for educational, non-commercial use. All copies must contain this notice. http://www.annettemackey.com

6 / 8 Time Additional Practice
Worksheet 4.2

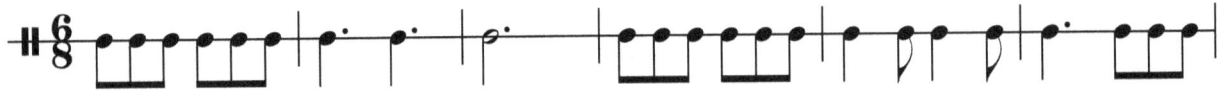

7

14
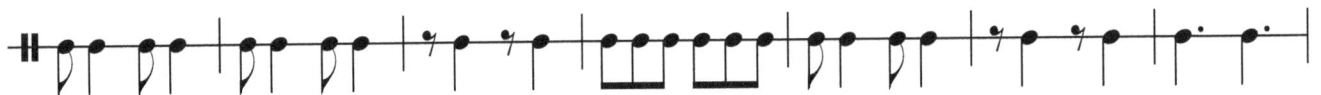

21

28

34
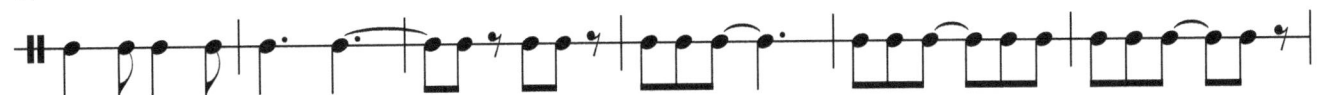

40

46
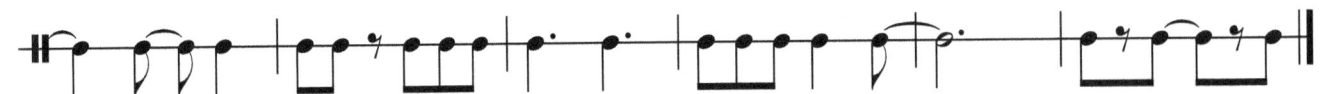

Copyright 2013 by Annette Mackey. AFTER INITIAL PURCHASE a copy may be made for educational, non-commercial use. All copies must contain this notice. http://www.annettemackey.com

6 / 8 Time Additional Practice
Worksheet 4.3

7

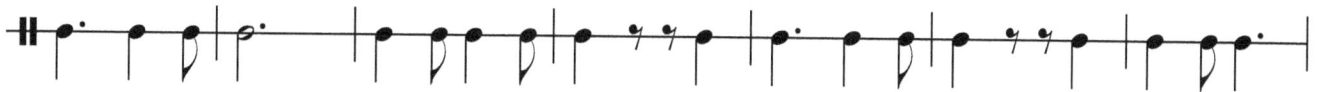

14

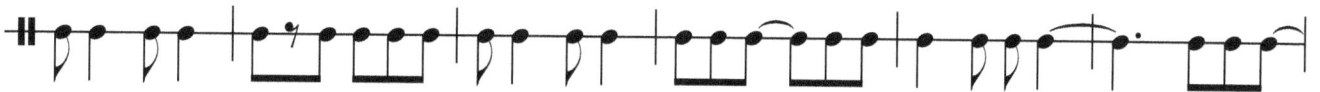

20

27

34

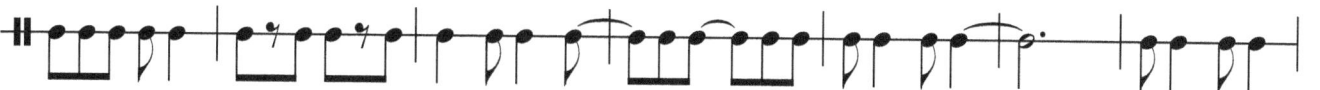

41

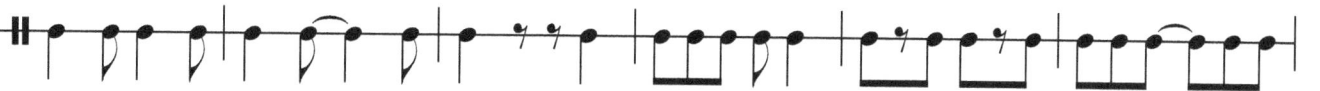

47

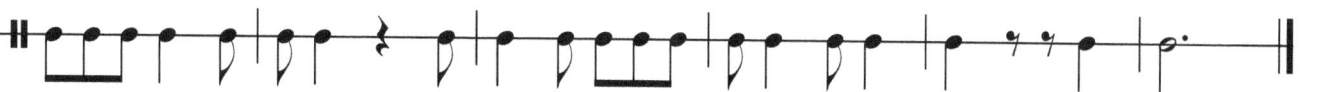

Copyright 2013 by Annette Mackey. AFTER INITIAL PURCHASE a copy may be made for educational, non-commercial use. All copies must contain this notice. http://www.annettemackey.com

6 / 8 Time Additional Practice
Worksheet 4.4

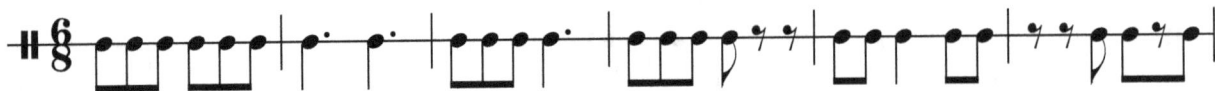

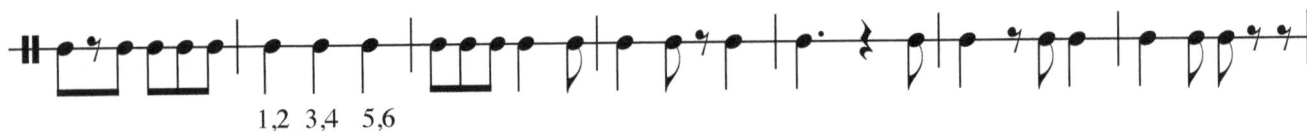

1,2 3,4 5,6

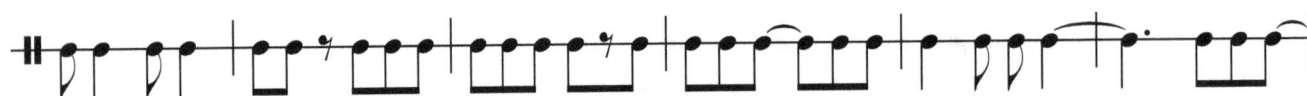

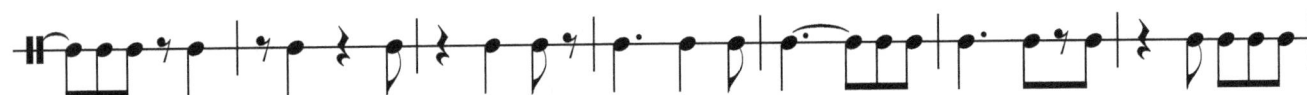

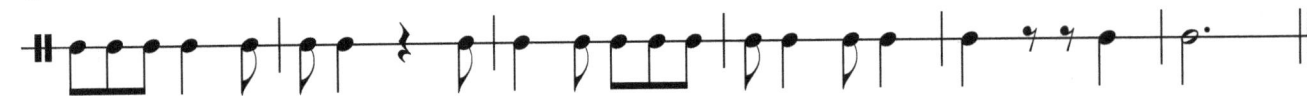

Copyright 2013 by Annette Mackey. AFTER INITIAL PURCHASE a copy may be made for educational, non-commercial use. All copies must contain this notice. http://www.annettemackey.com

Introducing 9 / 8 Time
Worksheet 4.5

Copyright 2013 by Annette Mackey. AFTER INITIAL PURCHASE a copy may be made for educational, non-commercial use. All copies must contain this notice. http://www.annettemackey.com

Introducing 9 / 8 Time
Worksheet 4.6

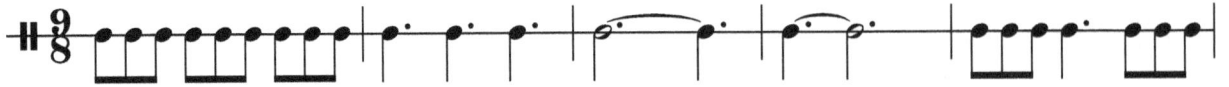

6

11

16

21

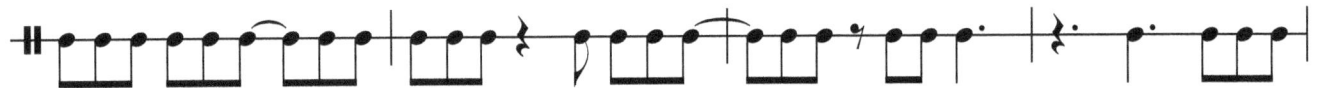

25

29

33

Copyright 2013 by Annette Mackey. AFTER INITIAL PURCHASE a copy may be made for educational, non-commercial use. All copies must contain this notice. http://www.annettemackey.com

Introducing 12 / 8 Time
Worksheet 4.7

Copyright 2013 by Annette Mackey. AFTER INITIAL PURCHASE a copy may be made for educational, non-commercial use. All copies must contain this notice. http://Twww.annettemackey.com

Introducing 12 / 8 Time
Worksheet 4.8

5
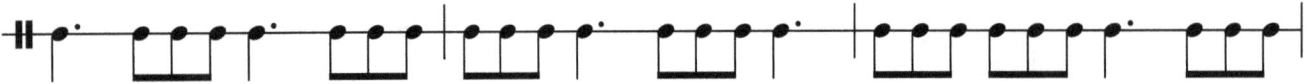

8

11

15

18

22
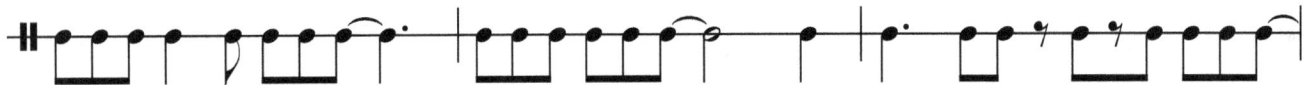

25

Copyright 2013 by Annette Mackey. AFTER INITIAL PURCHASE a copy may be made for educational, non-commercial use. All copies must contain this notice. http://www.annettemackey.com